DISGUSTING HISTORY

The Bloody, Rotten Roman Empire

THE DISGUSTING DETAILS ABOUT LIFE IN ANCIENT ROME

by James A. Corrick

raintree

a Capstone company — publishers for children

Raintree is an imprint of Capstone Global Library Limited, a company incorporated in England and Wales having its registered office at 7 Pilgrim Street, London, EC4V 6LB – Registered company number: 6695582

www.raintree.co.uk
myorders@raintree.co.uk

Edited by Mari Bolte
Designed by Alison Thiele and Gene Bentdahl
Picture research by Wanda Winch
Production by Eric Manske

ISBN 978 1 4747 1960 5
19 18 17 16 15
10 9 8 7 6 5 4 3 2 1

British Library Cataloguing in Publication Data
A full catalogue record for this book is available from the British Library

Photo Credits
Alamy: Lebrecht Music and Arts Photo Library, 7, North Wind Picture Archives, 26, World History Archive, 25, 27; The Art Archive: NGS Image Collection/H.M. Herget, 14 (top); The Bridgeman Art Library International: Index/Louvre, Paris, France, 21; Capstone: Chris Forsey, 5 (btm); Getty Images Inc: De Agostini Picture Library/De Agostini, 16, The Bridgeman Art Library International/Fedor Andreevich Bronnikov, 22, The Bridgeman Art Library International/Private Collection, 12; The Granger Collection, New York, 19 (top); iStockphoto: Alan Tobey, 14 (btm); Johnny Shumate, cover; Mary Evans Picture Library, 8, 23; North Wind Picture Archives, 11, 29; Nova Development Corporation, 4 (top right), 5 (top); Shutterstock: akva, 19 (btm), 26 (btm), Asier Villafrance, 4 (btm right), Dianna Toney, 4 (middle), freelanceartist, grunge design, ppl, 4 (btm left), Turi Tamas, Fact box design element

Primary Source Bibliography
Page 19—as published in *De Medicina* by Aulus Cornelius Celsus (Cambridge, Mass.: Harvard University Press, 1935–38).
Page 26—from *The Deeds of the Divine Augustus* by Augustus, as published in *The Gladiators: History's Most Deadly Sport* by Fik Meijer and translated by Liz Walters (New York: Thomas Dunne Books, 2005).

We would like to thank Richard S. Williams for his invaluable help in the preparation of this book.

Every effort has been made to contact copyright holders of material reproduced in this book. Any omissions will be rectified in subsequent printings if notice is given to the publisher.

All the internet addresses (URLs) given in this book were valid at the time of going to press. However, due to the dynamic nature of the internet, some addresses may have changed, or sites may have changed or ceased to exist since publication. While the author and publisher regret any inconvenience this may cause readers, no responsibility for any such changes can be accepted by either the author or the publisher.

Printed and bound in China

CONTENTS

ROME
753 BC — AD 476

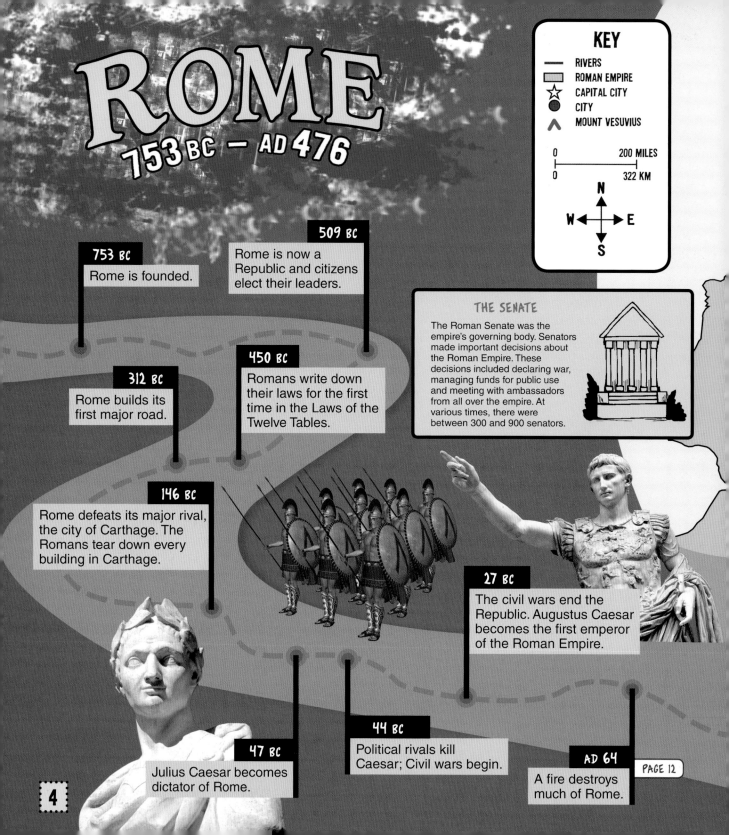

753 BC
Rome is founded.

509 BC
Rome is now a Republic and citizens elect their leaders.

312 BC
Rome builds its first major road.

450 BC
Romans write down their laws for the first time in the Laws of the Twelve Tables.

THE SENATE

The Roman Senate was the empire's governing body. Senators made important decisions about the Roman Empire. These decisions included declaring war, managing funds for public use and meeting with ambassadors from all over the empire. At various times, there were between 300 and 900 senators.

146 BC
Rome defeats its major rival, the city of Carthage. The Romans tear down every building in Carthage.

27 BC
The civil wars end the Republic. Augustus Caesar becomes the first emperor of the Roman Empire.

47 BC
Julius Caesar becomes dictator of Rome.

44 BC
Political rivals kill Caesar; Civil wars begin.

AD 64
A fire destroys much of Rome.

PAGE 12

4

BRITAIN

GAUL

ATLANTIC OCEAN

RIVER RHINE

RIVER DANUBE

ROMAN EMPIRE BY THE NUMBERS: AD 250

300 MILLION – number of people in the world

65 MILLION – number of people living under the rule of the Roman Empire

1.000.000 – number of people living in the city of Rome

500.000 – number of slaves living in the city of Rome

600 – number of senators

1 – number of emperors who ruled Rome

SPAIN

ITALY

CORSICA

R. TIBER

ADRIATIC SEA

ROME

POMPEII

SARDINIA

CONSTANTINOPLE

GREECE

SICILY

ATHENS

CARTHAGE

MEDITERRANEAN SEA

AD 80

PAGE 24

The Roman Colosseum opens.

AD 324

Constantinople founded as Eastern capital.

AD 476

The fall of Rome. Last western emperor overthrown.

AD 79

The volcano Mount Vesuvius destroys the Roman city of Pompeii.

AD 391

Christianity becomes the religion of Rome.

5

FILTHY STREETS

Two thousand years ago, the Roman Empire ruled all the lands that bordered the Mediterranean Sea. Romans had many tools that helped to make their lives easier. But there were also parts of Roman life that were dirty, unpleasant or even deadly.

The Romans grew rich from their empire. Gold, silver and other treasures flowed into Rome. There were large public buildings and many expensive homes. There was also a huge sporting arena and two racecourses.

But Rome was not all gold and riches. Rubbish filled the streets in the poorer parts of the city. There was also plenty of human and animal waste. Only the very rich had running water. Human waste piled up outside people's homes. Animals lived on the streets, dropping waste as they moved around.

Shops lined the streets of ancient Rome.

People killed animals for food in the street. The animal remains were thrown in the sewer.

FOUL FACT

Rome was a messy place. Citizens produced more than 50,000 kilograms (110,000 pounds) of solid waste every day.

Rome's sewers emptied into the nearby River Tiber. Rainwater washed the waste from the sewers into the river. There were big openings on the street for people to throw waste into the sewers. These holes let out the stench from beneath.

Few homes had toilets. Some people paid to use public toilets, which were set up over the sewers. Other people used chamber pots.

By law, Romans were supposed to empty their chamber pots into a sewer drain. But some people lived in tall buildings. They did not want to carry smelly pots down the many stairs to the drains. So they just emptied the pots out of their windows. People passing by were sometimes showered in waste.

There were laws against throwing bodily fluids from windows. Because there were no street lights, however, the laws were impossible to enforce at night.

The rubbish and animal waste mixed together in the streets. Everyone walked in this slimy mess. Workers were employed to keep the streets clean. But the sewage would always build up again.

The River Tiber was polluted with rubbish and human waste.

CITIZENS AND SLAVES

In Rome there were people who were free, and others who were slaves. Of those that were free, many were Roman citizens. Others were foreigners, merchants or diplomats.

Although Roman women were citizens, they had fewer rights than men. Women could own property. But they could not vote or hold government offices. Women had male **guardians** all their lives. The guardians were usually husbands or male relatives.

The wealthiest Roman citizens had power over the poor. Rich Romans bought and sold goods throughout the empire. They even bought and sold people.

Thousands of slaves worked in and around Rome. Slaves were bought and sold at auctions. There, they were undressed and kept in pens. This way, potential buyers could see for themselves whether or not slaves were healthy.

Some slaves were treated well. A few were paid, and some gained their freedom. But for most, life as a slave was horrible. Some slaves killed their babies at birth rather than allow them to become slaves.

guardian someone who carefully watches and protects another person

STORAX.SERVORV
MANGO

A white sign around a slave's neck told potential buyers everything they needed to know about the slave before buying.

Some owners branded or tattooed their slaves' faces. Other slaves were bound with heavy neck chains or collars so they could not escape. Some slaves had to wear tags that showed their masters' names.

There was nothing fair about the treatment of slaves. An owner could beat, torture or kill a slave for any reason. One Roman broke the legs of a slave who annoyed him. A slave who killed his owner was put to death. And so were all the other slaves in the household – men, women and children.

FOUL FACT

In AD 64, a fire swept through Rome. The city's wooden buildings fed the flames that burned for six days and seven nights.

EdONII·dICIT
ASSIdVS·HIC
dIdITVR

Many Romans ate their meals at food stands.

DEADLY HOMES

After a long day at work, imagine coming home to find three people sleeping in your bed! It might seem crowded, but Romans were used to it.

At one time, the city of Rome was home to more than 1 million people. In the city, most people lived in homes like flats, above shops. The poorest people shared rooms on the highest storeys. Some buildings were eight or nine storeys high. These buildings were not safe. The ground floor and first floor might be made of sturdy stone. But the higher storeys were often made only of mud and wood. Many buildings fell under their own weight. Those unlucky enough to be in a building when it collapsed often died.

These buildings also burned down. Although cooking inside the homes was discouraged, some people did it anyway. Unattended flames from lamps or cooking fires could lead to disaster. The buildings were built with mud bricks and timber that caught fire easily and burned quickly. There were no fire alarms or fire escapes. People on the highest floors often died.

Building owners rarely cared about these deaths. One owner was actually happy that one of his buildings collapsed. He planned to rebuild and charge higher rents.

Rich Romans ate lying down.

FOUL FACT

Guests at a Roman feast might snack on grasshoppers, grubs or animal parts.

NASTY MEALS

Imagine arriving at a friend's house for dinner. Instead of pizza and salad, you're served snails and pig's stomach! Romans didn't go to restaurants or supermarkets to buy their food. Food came from farms all over the empire.

Most Romans ate simple meals. The poorest ate bread or porridge with vegetables. Those with more money sometimes had fish. Few Romans ate meat, which was too expensive.

The wealthy, of course, ate well. They threw special feasts that lasted for hours. Some Romans spent all their money trying to impress their friends.

The hosts served strange food. Unusual dishes at these feasts included ostrich or peacock. Animal tongue and brains were eaten. Sometimes mice were used as stuffing for birds or other animals. A favourite dish was a small bird called the figpecker. Guests ate all parts of this bird except for its beak.

Both rich and poor Romans used olive oil for cooking and flavouring. But even more popular was garum. This sauce was made from aged fish heads, fins and guts. It was poured over most foods and even used as a medicine.

GRASSHOPPERS

KEEPING CLEAN

It's time for a bath – with 1,500 other people! Being clean was important to Romans. Many people bathed daily at public bathhouses. They sat in warm pools or steam rooms. While soaking, people caught up with friends and discussed business. Men and women bathed at different times.

There were hot or cold baths. Wood fires, below the baths, were burned by slaves to heat the water. **Aqueducts** brought in 750,000 litres (198,130 gallons) of fresh spring water a day.

Romans did not have soap. Instead, they rubbed themselves with olive oil. Then they scraped themselves clean with a curved metal tool. The oil helped to remove dirt.

aqueduct bridge built to carry water

Without soap, Romans had to find other ways to clean their clothes. They found a way of cleaning clothes using human urine. To collect the urine, laundry workers set out pots in the street. Roman men would relieve themselves into these pots. The dirty clothes were soaked and scrubbed in vats of urine.

The baths and laundries did not keep the Romans safe from fleas and lice. Dirty streets and homes meant that the number of pests was high. Romans had no way to rid themselves of these annoying creatures. People tried getting rid of fleas and lice by rubbing themselves with animal fat or drinking a concoction that included bits of dead skin.

FOUL FACT

The emperors Nero and Vespasian put a tax on urine. The urine was collected from pots and then sold, usually to laundries or leather shops.

DISEASE AND DOCTORS

Romans were in constant danger from sickness and infection. Roman doctors, who did not understand what caused disease, could do little to stop outbreaks. Many people caught **malaria**. Sometimes people got **smallpox**. Thousands became sick and died every year. Only 50 per cent of children survived to become adults.

Do you have a headache? Why not try some goat dung soup? That was just one of the many remedies Romans used. Roman doctors had a wide variety of medicines, which were mainly herbal. But there were many treatments that did not work. Romans routinely took pills made from dried insects or crushed-up snakes. Swellings were packed with animal waste.

Many doctors were self-taught. In fact, any man with some tools and herbs could claim he was a doctor. While there were a number of good doctors, there were also many frauds. Romans who were poor did not have the luxury of choosing who treated them.

malaria serious disease that people catch from mosquito bites

smallpox contagious disease that causes chills, fever and spots that scar

Pain and the doctor

Now a surgeon should be youthful ... with a strong and steady hand which never trembles ... with vision sharp and clear, and spirit undaunted; filled with pity, so that he wishes to cure his patient, yet is not moved by his cries, to go too fast, or cut less than is necessary; but he does everything just as if the cries of pain cause him no emotion.

Aulus Cornelius Celsus
Doctor and author of De Medicina

Certain animals were sacrificed to each god. Bulls, rams and boars were acceptable gifts for gods.

sacrifice offering, or gift, made to a god

altar large table used for religious ceremonies

BLOODY SACRIFICES

The Romans worshipped many gods and goddesses. Popular gods were Jupiter and his wife, Juno. Mars and Venus also had many followers. Rulers often claimed gods or goddesses as their ancestors.

Romans made **sacrifices** to important gods. It was hoped that the gods would be pleased with these gifts. The most common sacrifice was a goat or a cow. A priest would kill the animal and would search the liver for messages from the gods. Then he burned the liver, fat, guts and bones on the god's **altar**. After the ceremony, the Romans cooked and ate the rest of the animal.

Roman families had their own household gods. These gods were thought to protect the family from harm. They were given gifts of grain or wine and received part of a family's meal.

Romans held many official religious events throughout the year. In the middle of February, priests sacrificed several goats and a dog to the god Pan. This celebration was held to represent the founding of Rome. In October, Romans would hold the October Horse, a chariot race held in honour of the god Mars. A priest killed one of the winning horses and cut off its head. Two teams fought over the head, which was thought to bring good luck.

CRIME AND PUNISHMENT

Romans who broke the law could end up losing their lives. There were many types of punishment, but being sent to prison was not one of them. The Romans used prisons only to hold prisoners before their trial or punishment.

Citizens could not be given physical punishment for minor crimes such as **forgery** or lying. Instead, guilty citizens might have to pay a fine or leave Rome. Sometimes they were sent to live alone on small islands. Those who committed major crimes, such as **treason** or murder, might have their heads cut off. Others could be thrown from a cliff known as Tarpeian Rock.

Non-citizens faced harsher punishments, such as being whipped. The Roman whip had three strands of leather. Each strand was braided with lead balls or sharp pieces of metal. It was sometimes used to beat a criminal to death.

forgery crime of making illegal copies of paintings, money or other valuable objects

treason act of betraying one's country

Death was the penalty for crimes such as treason, murder, theft and arson. Arsonists were burned alive. Another way of carrying out the death sentence was being tied or nailed to a wooden cross. The victim often died slowly and painfully. Only foreigners and slaves could be whipped to death, burned alive or hung on a cross.

People who committed crimes against Rome were thrown off Tarpeian Rock.

Hanging from a cross was considered the most disgraceful way to die.

DEADLY SPORTS

Romans enjoyed deadly sports. Competitors entered the arena knowing they might not leave alive. Emperors and other rich citizens paid to organize the games. Arenas such as the Colosseum attracted audiences from all around Rome. More than 50,000 people packed the Colosseum to watch these deadly contests.

Most gladiators were either slaves or prisoners of war. But a few were citizens who fought for respect. Just like today's professional athletes, successful gladiators received star treatment, and were adored by the crowds of spectators.

Gladiators experienced tough training at special schools. Fighters pledged to endure humiliation and death without protest. But, for some, gladiator school seemed like a good option. They were fed three meals a day, received medical care and had the chance to win fame and money. If they survived long enough, they could even win their freedom.

FOUL FACT

The bodies of people and smaller animals killed at the Colosseum were often dumped into the River Tiber.

Gladiators were expected to fight bravely, and to die with honour.

In the morning, wild animals battled each other or armed men inside the arena. Planners of the games travelled far and wide to find wild animals for the Colosseum. Animals such as rhinos and bears were brought in from great distances. Many animals were killed in the Colosseum.

In the afternoon, criminals condemned to death were brought in to fight. Sometimes they were pitted against each other. At other times, they battled trained gladiators. The criminals rarely won. The winner's prize was to keep fighting to the death.

A hunting show organized by the general Pompey featured 20 elephants, 600 lions and more than 400 leopards.

Animals in the arena

Three times I held gladiator games in my own name and five times in the name of my sons or grandsons. During the games, around 10,000 men fought each other to the death … Twenty-six times I presented the people with hunting shows with wild animals from Africa … and in them around 3,500 animals were killed.

Emperor Augustus (27 BC-AD 14)
From The Deeds of the Divine Augustus

Deaths were common at the Circus Maxiumus.

Romans took their games to racecourses, too. There were several racecourses throughout Rome. The Circus Maximus was the most popular. It could seat 100,000 spectators. Chariots pulled by four horses were a favourite with the crowds.

Horses raced around at full speed. They raced for 7 laps, which was 8 kilometres (5 miles). There were sharp turns at the corners and frequent crashes. Drivers were sometimes dragged to their deaths. They could also be crushed under hooves or wheels.

BATTLE WOUNDS

Soldiers in the Roman army had a tough life. It was the army's job to protect Rome from attack. There was no room for failure, and punishments were harsh. New recruits and the weakest soldiers were placed at the frontline during battles. This position helped them to gain more experience. It also prevented them from running away in fear.

Battle wounds were nasty. The soldiers fought with swords and spears. They also carried large shields. Both Roman and enemy weapons sliced deep into arms and legs. A strong blow from a sword could split a soldier's head open. Spears could cause fatal wounds.

Roman military training was hard. Being beaten with thick sticks was a common punishment. Sometimes a commanding officer ordered a soldier beaten to death. Occasionally the soldier's head was cut off afterwards. When large groups of soldiers deserted, the punishment was harsh. The commanding officer selected every tenth man. The other soldiers then beat the selected men until they died.

Whether you were a soldier, gladiator, slave or citizen, life was dirty, disgusting and deadly in ancient Rome!

Roman soldiers fought their enemies at close range.

GLOSSARY

altar large table used for religious ceremonies

aqueduct bridge built to carry water

forgery crime of making illegal copies of paintings, money or other valuable objects

guardian someone who carefully watches and protects another person

malaria serious disease that people catch from mosquito bites

sacrifice gift of something valuable given to honour a god

smallpox contagious disease that causes chills, fever and spots that scar

treason act of betraying one's country

READ MORE

Ancient Rome (Technology in the Ancient World), Charlie Samuels (Franklin Watts, 2015)

Daily Life in Ancient Rome (Daily Life in Ancient Civilizations), Don Nardo (Raintree, 2015)

Roman Myths and Legends (All About Myths), Jilly Hunt (Raintree, 2013)

WEBSITES

www.bbc.co.uk/schools/primaryhistory/romans/
Find out more about Roman life.

www.dkfindout.com/uk/history/ancient-rome
Discover facts about life in ancient Rome.

INDEX